DAYS AT THE CO

by
Robert Preston

The legendary banana boat I didn't come up the Clyde on.

To Rita on our Ruby Anniversary Year

© Copyright 1994 Robert Preston
First Published in the United Kingdom, 1994
By Richard Stenlake, Ochiltree Sawmill, The Lade,
Ochiltree, Ayrshire, KA18 2NX
Telephone 01290 700266

Introduction

The trip doon the watter has long been a tradition in Glasgow and the west of Scotland. This means sailing out to the mouth of the Firth. After all, the Clyde was Glasgow's Riviera and Coney Island rolled into one.

Holidaymakers came out from Glasgow, Renfrew, Paisley, Kilmarnock and all the surrounding industrial towns filling up the boarding houses and small hotels in Gourock, Largs, Millport, Ayr, Rothesay, Dunoon and Helensburgh. For most people this annual trip was their one dose of fresh air. Even the trip to the resort was an adventure. For most holidaymakers it began with a boat trip on one of the multitude of different paddle steamers that sailed from Glasgow and all points further down the Clyde.

My story will take the reader on a journey from Glasgow past docks, shipyards, ferries and places of interest doon the watter. Reaching Wemyss Bay the Clyde opens out and the choice is vast. From the Cloch Lighthouse it is possible to cross the Firth to visit Bute and Argyll or turn southward to follow the Renfrewshire coast on the way to all those Ayrshire resorts. Turning right takes you up to Helensburgh, the other Dunbartonshire resorts and the starting point for trips to Loch Lomond. Leaving Glasgow by train it was possible to connect direct with the many pierheads on the Clyde as well as many of the resorts.

This book is about the people, places and ships that helped make the Fair Holiday a happy memory for millions. Only the Waverley remains now of the hundreds of famous paddle steamers that plied the Clyde and serves as a reminder of happy trips doon the watter and visits to all the Clyde coast resorts.

Robert Preston, September 1994

Glasgow Fair Saturday at Dunoon.

Advertised by Waverley Excursions Ltd, in association with the Paddle Steamer Preservation Society, as the last sea-going paddle steamer in the world, the Waverley still travels to many of the places mentioned in this book. She was built by A.J. Inglis (Glasgow) in 1946 for the London & North Eastern Railway and used on the Lochgoilhead and Arrochar run from Craigendoran. Transferred to the Caledonian Steam Packet Company in November 1951 she subsequently operated on most of their routes.

Withdrawn in 1973, Waverley was sold by Caledonian MacBrayne to the Society for £1 and re-entered Clyde service in 1975. Since that date she has been a regular sight in the Clyde as well as many ports of call elsewhere in Britain.

The top picture shows the third ship to carry the name Waverley, built in 1899 at Inglis' yard at Pointhouse. She was requisitioned in both World Wars and was bombed at Dunkirk in 1940.

Below is the fourth Waverley passing West Bay, Dunoon on her first sailing on the 6th of June 1947. As originally built, she could carry 1350 passengers and her engines could push her to 15 knots.

The Clyde and its holidaymakers have known many ships down through the years that their names have probably been forgotten. But mention the Queen Mary and I am sure that many will have happy memories of the daily sail from Bridge Wharf on the south side.

Built by Denny's of Dumbarton and launched on March 30th, 1933, the Queen Mary made her first public sail in May of that year. A name change came about in 1934 with the launching of a new Cunarder also called the Queen Mary. Her owners, Williamson-Buchanan renamed her Queen Mary II and it wasn't until 1976 that she dropped the II and reclaimed her rightful name.

It seems ironic that during the period leading up to this change Williamson-Buchanan were offering trips to 'view the 70,000 ton Cunard White Star liner now under construction at Clydebank. This vessel, the largest in the world, is expected to be launched on Wednesday 26th September by Her Majesty the Queen'.

The top view shows the Queen Mary leaving Dunoon in her wartime livery. During World War Two the Queen Mary II was sometimes used as a tender for troopships loading in the Clyde. Below is P.S. Kylemore passing the great Cunarder Queen Mary at Clydebank in the early 1930s.

4

LET GLASGOW FLOURISH

Once a year, Glasgow damps down her furnaces and heads for the coast. It is her Fair and in mid July a swarm of citizens converge on the Firth's many tourist resorts. In the past, Glasgow's pall of smoke rolled back and as the air altered and grew clean, it was once again possible to see the dear green place. Nowadays, there are few factories belching out smoke and soot.

These two views sum it all up and were issued as postcards in 1903-4.

GLASGOW STILL FLOURISHING

P. S. "Isle of Arran" leaving Broomielaw.
Saloon Steamers "Isle of Arran", "Isle of Bute" and "Isle of Cumbrae" sail daily from Broomielaw at 10 and 11 a. m. (Sundays 11 a. m.) for Dunoon, Rothesay, Kyles of Bute etc. during the Season. For particulars see Glasgow newspapers.

The Isle of Arran was built at Rutherglen in 1892. It seems unlikely that a shipyard could exist so far up river but T.B. Seath's produced many small ships last century with this being the last. The Isle of Arran was used on the Arran routes as well as to Rothesay and the Kyles of Bute. During World War One she was requisitioned as a mine sweeper and returned safely. After a refit, she lasted on the Clyde till 1933. For another three years she worked on the Thames and was then scrapped.

In addition to the cross river ferries for both passengers and vehicles, there was a service of passenger boats travelling up and down the upper reaches of the Clyde. Originally the routes from Glasgow to Whiteinch and Govan were operated by horse buses. With a high fare of 4d there was an opening for a cheaper mode of transport. The small boats, called Clutha 1 to 12, were carrying between two and three million passengers a year by the 1890s from their landing stage at the Broomielaw. The Cluthas were themselves killed off by competition from the electric tramcars (introduced in 1898). As the trams moved westward the Cluthas succumbed and the final service of the penny boats ran in November 1903.

The harbour of Glasgow was fully two and a half miles long. Originally the Clyde had been too shallow for anything except the smallest of boats, but a concerted effort was made over many years to narrow and deepen the channel so that larger ships could travel up the Clyde to Glasgow. As a greater depth of water was attained, additional quays were constructed on both sides of the river. Kingston was the first of Glasgow's great docks and opened in 1867. Thirteen years later Queens Dock opened, followed by Princes Dock in 1900 and Rothesay Dock at Clydebank in 1907.

During their visit of 1907, the Prince of Wales and Princess Alexandra opened the Rothesay Dock. The new dock was originally to be called the Clydebank Dock but the Clyde Trustees agreed to a name change in honour of the Royal visitors. The opening ceremony was performed aboard the Caledonian Steam Packet Company's paddle steamer Duchess of Rothesay.

ROTHESAY DOCK, CLYDEBANK.

H.M. Yacht "Victoria & Albert" with their Majesties on board, steaming around the Fleet on the Clyde. July 10th 1920.

Other Royal visitors to the Clyde were King George V and Queen Mary. They came to take part in the Royal Northern Yacht Club Regatta and sailed to the Clyde on the Steam Yacht Victoria and Albert. Atrocious weather marred the visit, but the King took part in the Regatta and won his race in the yacht Britannia.

H.M.S. "Argus" manned for the purpose of cheering their Majesties on the occasion of the latter's visit to the Clyde. July 10th 1920.

The Fleet was berthed in the Clyde and their Majesties steamed round the many great battleships including the aircraft carrier HMS Argus.

Water Row, Govan was on the way to the ferry across to Partick. The hand operated wagon ferry was replaced in 1867 by a steam powered boat. This ferry hauled itself from one side to the other by pulling itself along a heavy chain laid on the river bed. The Govan - Partick ferry ceased to operate in 1965.

Across from Water Row was Inglis' Pointhouse shipyard. Many of the Clyde steamers were built here, including both Waverleys. Also near the mouth of the Kelvin was the Pointhouse Inn which was managed by the Clyde Trustees and demolished in 1909.

Partick Pier. RELIABLE SERIES.

Fifteen minutes after leaving the Broomielaw, Partick Pier was the next call for the paddlers. In this picture the Caledonia has just called on its way to Rothesay. The first ship built for the Caledonian Steam Packet Company at Port Glasgow in 1889, her top speed was just over sixteen knots. She lasted until 1933 when she was scrapped at Barrow in Furness.

Largest Crane in the World. Height 170 ft. Length of Jib 258 ft. Lifting Capacity 250 tons. Fairfield Shipbuilding Yard, Govan.

On the left one could see Fairfield Shipyard. To lift some of the massive steel sections needed for shipbuilding, the yard had the largest crane in the world and during busy periods employed between six and seven thousand people.

Copeland, Tuskar and Lizard are three of the boats visible in this September, 1907 view of the docks at Kingston.

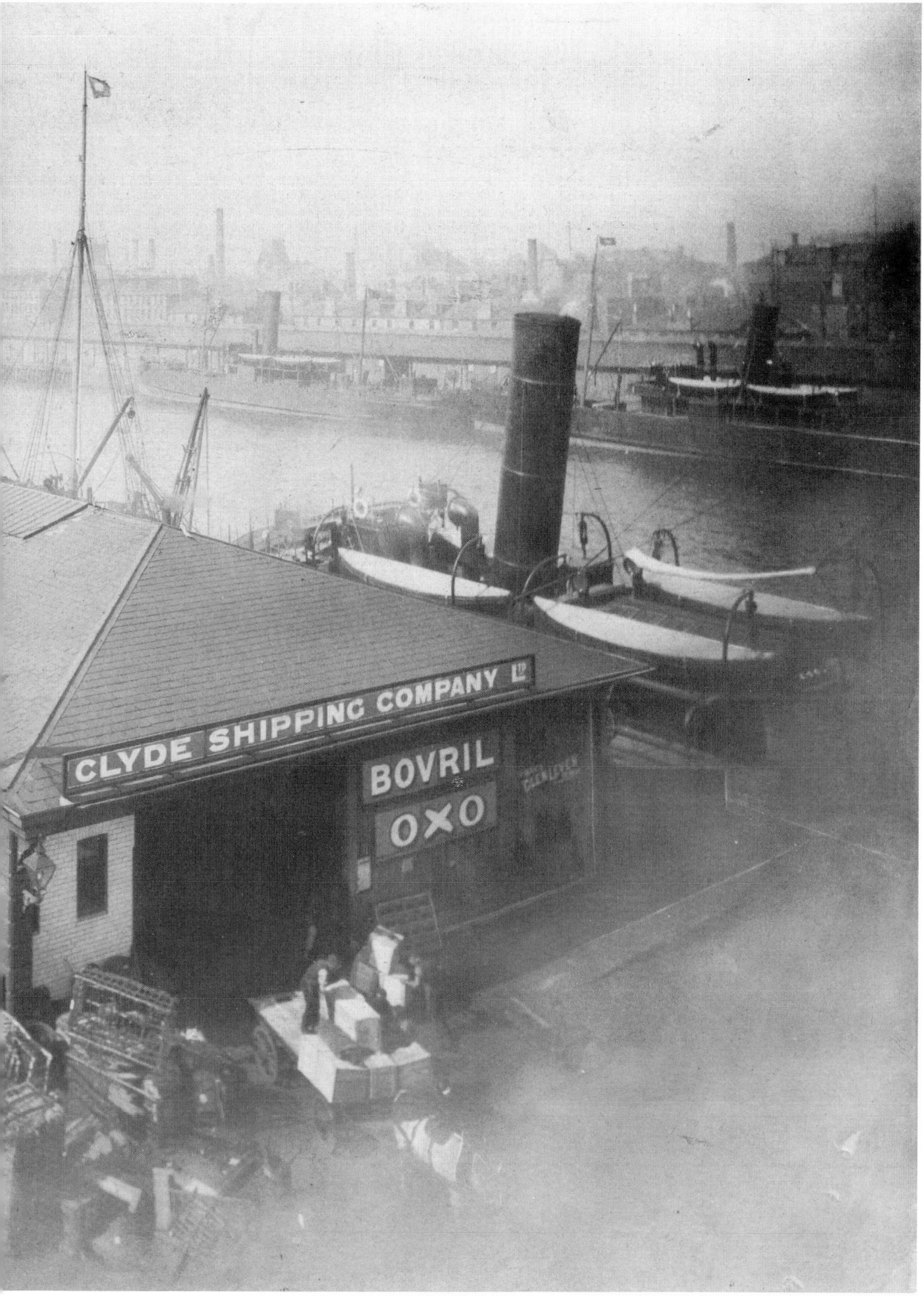
CLYDE SHIPPING COMPANY L^TD
BOVRIL
OXO

The double chain ferry seen here was constructed in 1897. Vehicles would use the centre section, while passengers were accommodated round the sides. It was sold in 1936 for service at Kessock between Inverness and the Black Isle. Unfortunately, it was too wide for the locks on the Caledonian Canal and, as a result, was dismantled. In the background of the top picture is the Isle of Cumbrae with what looks like a full complement of over 1000 passengers. The Isle of Cumbrae was originally called the Jeanie Deans and was owned by the North British Railway. She went through a few owners before being bought by Buchanan in 1904. She was scrapped in 1920. Below is the Isle of Arran.

The building of the two Queen Elizabeths and the Queen Mary made John Brown's the best known of all the Clyde shipbuilders. Former owners J & G Thomson (1847-97) were restructured following a depression in their final year and became the Clydebank Shipbuilding & Engineering Company. Ownership passed to John Brown, a firm of Sheffield steelmakers, in 1899.

The Aquitania about to pass the Henry Bell Monument at Bowling. She was thought to be one of the most beautiful liners built on the Clyde and sailed for many years as one of the most prestigious Cunarders.

S.S. "LUSITANIA" (TURBINE) LENGTH 780 FEET, BUILT BY JOHN BROWN & CO, LTD, CLYDEBANK, FOR CUNARD STEAMSHIP CO.

The Lusitania was launched in June 1906, but didn't leave on her maiden voyage until September 1907. It was the sinking of the Lusitania in 1915 that eventually brought the Americans into World War One. She was sunk off the coast of Ireland by a German submarine with a great loss of life.

TURBINE STEAMER "ATALANTA" AT LARGS PIER

The Atalanta was built at the same time as the Lusitania and its turbine engines were a small scale version of those fitted to the Lusitania. She was the fourth turbine steamer on the Clyde and was used mainly on the winter run from Ardrossan to Arran. She was also used for excursions and was sometimes seen as far away as Stranraer. In 1937 she was sold to new owners in Lancashire. After five years war service, Atalanta was scrapped at Ghent in 1947.

Erskine Ferry, Old Kilpatrick

A few miles past Renfrew is Erskine. This small village has a long history as a crossing point on the Clyde. The ferry boat shown here is probably the single chain Govan Ferry No.2. Dating from 1867, this boat could carry three horses and carts in the central carriageway with 50 passengers. In 1875 this boat became a reserve boat and was reported as working at Erskine.

Erskine No.1 was a double chain steam ferry built in 1903. In 1935 the ferry was replaced by a two funneled boat and sold for service at Kessock Ferry, but sank off Campbeltown while being towed to its new home.

On the right is Bowling. The Clyde pleasure fleets lay at anchor here for the winter and in this view at least four are visible.

The pier dates from about 1848 and became an important link with the railway, particularly the line to Balloch and Loch Lomond. The steamer shown here is Buchanan's Isle of Cumbrae returning from its tour of the Clyde. Originally called Jeanie Deans, she was sold off the Clyde in 1896 and saw service in Londonderry for two years before returning as the Duchess of York. Bought by Buchanan in 1904, her name was changed to Isle of Cumbrae.

A Blue Star cargo ship passes the harbour at Bowling where two paddlers are berthed for the winter.

Bowling was well served with all forms of transport. This view shows the railway, canal, road and River Clyde. The Forth and Clyde was finished in 1790 from Grangemouth to Bowling and was extended to Port Dundas in the same year. It closed in 1963 but the locks and basins at Bowling still remain in use today.

The railway to Greenock opened in 1841 and bought a share of two paddle steamers in the same year. As a result of this, the railway was in a position to offer through rail and steamer connections to eight Clyde resorts. It took less than an hour to reach Greenock by train while the boats took two to three hours depending on the tide. A price war started and this led to a massive upsurge in traffic volumes. This railway was owned by the Caledonian Railway and it tried to keep the Glasgow & South Western Railway out of its territory, but the policy failed and the line to Princes Pier opened in 1869. In this view one of the Caledonian steamers sits at the West Quay in Greenock.

Competition was severe and prices fell as both railways tried to gain the traffic. Passengers travelling by the Glasgow & South Western had an advantage as the trains called at Princes Pier. Those using the Caledonian had to walk from the station to Custom House Quay. The boats called at both piers and the Caledonian slowed the trains down at their station so that the boats would be delayed and the passengers would be left waiting at Princes Pier. The Caley lost its mail contract because of this and passenger numbers declined. Eventually the companies came to an agreement and split the revenues.

Also from Princes Pier the Anchor Line of steamers embarked their passengers to America and Canada. Many travelled from Glasgow on special trains.

Gourock was the earliest watering place on the Clyde and the place where red herrings were first cured. It was also the place from which James IV set sail to assert his authority over the Western Isles in 1594.

Old Granny Kempoch, Gourock

Near the pier can be seen Granny Kempoch, an ancient stone which mariners used to perform certain rites around to secure favourable winds for their voyages.

WEMYSS BAY STATION. 832/39.

After its problems with Greenock, the Caledonian Railway improved its line and service to Wemyss Bay. This culminated in the construction of the majestic railway station which opened in 1903. It was designed by James Miller, the Railway's own architect. Its glass roof and impressive frontage make it one of Scotland's architectural treasures. Floral decoration was always much in evidence and, when opened, advertisements within the buildings were confined to those of the railway and the Caledonian Steam Packet Company.

The steamer at the pier is the Duchess of Montrose. Built in 1902 at John Brown's, her capacity was 1221 passengers. Originally built to operate from Ayr in competition with the Juno, she spent most of her life on general duties. Requisitioned in 1914, her life was cut short by a mine and she sank off Belgium in 1917.

Pictured sometime about 1910, the Glasgow & South Western Railway's Jupiter is just about to pass HMS Collingwood. At this time, the Home Fleet was a common sight in the Clyde.

During 1835 a wooden jetty was constructed at Dunoon. Prior to this visitors were landed by small ferry boats. As the tourist trade and boats grew in size, it became necessary to build a proper pier. In 1867 Mr Hunter of Halton House financed its construction. Further developments by Dunoon Town Council took place in 1898. The new buildings were opened by Lord and Lady Poltalloch and included sumptuous new waiting rooms.

In the background is the signalling tower. The first pierhead loudspeaker system on the Clyde was introduced here in 1934. This gave both the public and ships masters the berth numbers from which ships left and was used until the 1970s. The pier master at Dunoon for many years was Joe (Admiral) Beattie who allegedly charged his wife pier dues as well as dues for the verandah deck!

One holidaymaker in July 1925 sent the following message to a friend: "We left Glasgow at 10.40 by train for Gourock via Paisley, Kilmacolm, Port Glasgow and Greenock. By steamer we sailed six miles across the Firth of Clyde calling at Hunter's Quay at the foot of the Holy Loch, then Kirn and finally Dunoon. It is a lovely place. The nicest seaside resort I've seen up here. A strong sea breeze is blowing up the Firth of Clyde. The Clyde is two miles across to the nearest land (Cloch Point Lighthouse) and looking south it is open sea.

Dunoon is formed of East Bay (where we are - 30 seconds from front) and West Bay. We sailed on the Duchess of Fife. The boat up Loch Lomond was Princess May. Shall be meeting Sir Harry I expect".

The Princess May was assembled at Balloch from a huge kit of parts and put into service on Loch Lomond offering trips from one end to the other and calling at many of the small villages on the loch-side.

Laudervale, a house at Bullwood, Dunoon was bought by Sir Harry Lauder and his wife Annie during 1908. Originally called Gerhallow House, its name was changed in 1912. In 1934 they departed from Dunoon for Lauder Ha' at Strathaven and a farewell dinner was held in their honour.

Laudervale became a private hotel and its end came at 2.10am on the 28th March 1962 when the building was gutted by fire. The new owner, a heavy smoker, had fallen asleep and the building set alight. He died in the ensuing conflagration and two firemen were injured.

The Pavilion in Dunoon was opened in 1905 at a cost of £15,000. Concerts were given every afternoon and evening and there was seating for up to 2500 people. During wet weather the Pavilion was an ideal alternative to strolling around the nearby Castle Gardens. It burned down in April 1949.

Approaching the pier at Dunoon is Redgauntlet while already berthed is the Duchess of Hamilton. The Redgauntlet belonged to the North British Railway and was used on their services from Craigendoran. She was nearly lost off Arran in 1899 after being holed on some rocks. After being run aground, the passengers were rescued by the Waverley. Redgauntlet was given first aid and taken to Pointhouse for repairs. In 1909 she was transferred to the Firth of Forth and operated from Leith. After being bought by the Admiralty, she was sold to French owners who registered her in Oran, Algeria.

On a wet or tiring day spent on the beach with the weans, the holidaymaker could escape to Argyle Street for a couple of hours relaxation. The cinemas in Argyle Street were the La Scala and the Picture House. Argyle Street's most prominent building was, however, the Argyll Hotel.

Looking down to the Pier, this early 1900s view shows a teeming Argyll Street.

Cowal Highland Gathering held at Dunoon annually on Glasgow Trades holiday.

The Cowal Highland Games are held annually on the last Friday and Saturday of August and are 100 years old in 1994. Steamers and buses would have swelled the population of Dunoon as they brought many thousands of people to watch the annual event. World Championship Piping, dancing, hammer throwing, wrestling and tossing the caber were and still are some of the attractions. By 1929 the organisers were advertising 1000 pipers and the event had been filmed for cinema use.

Cowal Highland Gathering held at Dunoon annually on Glasgow Trades holiday

From Brown's 'Guide to Watering Places of the Clyde' (1862) comes the following description of Hunter's Quay and Kirn:

"Situated along the coast at the mouth of Holy Loch is the watering place named Hunter's Quay. From this point stretching along the road to Kirn - two miles distant - villa succeeds villa. There is a good pier at Kirn and it being easily approached from Glasgow by rail and steamer in one hour and a half, enjoys a large share of patronage. Along the shore for two miles towards Dunoon, cottages, villas and mansions are placed thickly."

On the south side of the Holy Loch, opposite Kilmun, lies Sandbank or Ardnadam. In 1800 the Government erected a lazaretto (quarantine station) here suited to receiving infected goods of every description. Fortunately for the existence of Sandbank and other holiday resorts, the plague ships with their sinister yellow flags no longer round Lazaretto Point and anchor there.

The railway bill boards on display at the entrance to the pier show the great choice on offer to the discerning traveller. The steamer calling is the Marchioness of Lorne.

The village of Kilmun stands on the north side of Holy Loch, four miles by water from Dunoon. The modern story of Kilmun starts with David Napier, the engineer, building an inn and some houses, followed by a road from Kilmun to Loch Eck. With his steam carriage running on the road and little steamer Aglaia on the Loch, he opened up the route to Inverary and the West Highlands.

Redgauntlet at Kilmun Pier circa 1904.

R.M.S. Columba leaving Innellan

The fears and realities of the Great War are expressed in these two pictures. The fear is expressed in the message of the top card dated 12th August, 1914. The war is a week old as the sender talks about contemporary news!

"Now the scare has died down things are nearly normal. The weather took up on Sunday and is grand now for sailing. I wrote W.H. that Loch Lomond tour was off but since found that it was only the Caledonian; North British running as usual - was on Monday anyhow. Hasn't it been a time for fairy tales, Germans everywhere. Hope you are managing without me, thinking of volunteering for the front (not much)."

The lower card shows the reality of the war. The Clyde Boom is in place. Stretching across the Clyde from Castle Rocks to the Cloch, ensuring that no enemy submarines could enter the river.

The Great War affected Clydeside greatly. Many of the paddlers were called into war service as minesweepers, troop transports and tenders. After six years of war service and lack of maintenance many paddle steamers were fit only for scrap. A rush of new building took place in the early 1920s to replace the worn out paddle steamers.

The "Clyde Boom" between Dunoon & Clochlight house

One generally associates camps at the seaside as places of fun and pleasure but I am afraid the opposite applies to the picture illustrated here. Glenbranter Estate situated at Strachur is now owned by the Forestry Commission but once belonged to a member of the MacBrayne family. Later it was bought by Sir Harry Lauder as a gift for his son. During the period 1933-34 the tenant appears to have been the Ministry of Labour which was using the area for the unemployed during the Depression. During the Second World War Glenbranter was a large prisoner of war camp. Soldiers who had survived Dunkirk guarded the camp. The house was demolished in 1956.

This post card comes from an internee - Rudolph R. Meyer - and was posted at Liverpool on 12th July, 1940. Being so early in the war, it seems likely that Rudolph Meyer was not a serviceman but more likely an immigrant. With the card being posted at Liverpool, he may have been on his way to the Isle of Man, which housed many of the immigrants who had escaped from Hitler's Germany before the war but who were nevertheless considered a security risk. In the message he asks for part of his wages to be used for debts for papers and cigarettes and for the remainder to be sent to Glenbranter.

The following pages show some of the sights one would have seen on the Loch Eck Coaching Tour. This would have taken the Edwardian tourist from Dunoon pierhead past the Argyll Hotel to Inveraray via the Holy Loch, Loch Eck and Strachur. The trips left daily at 10.30am.

Loch Eck Coach.

Having come off the Lord of the Isles, the sender of this 1903 post card probably bought it from the driver or guide. It was posted at Inveraray and sent to Cove.

33

The variety of steamer tours was almost endless. Those coming off the Lord of the Isles at Dunoon could travel by horse drawn coach and then on to the Fairy Queen on Loch Eck. This was a small pleasure steamer that had its own post office on board. All mail posted on the ship was stamped with a special purple cachet. The small boat only carried a few passengers and as a result there is very little mail surviving with this postmark.

Strachur Pier. (Lochfyne.)

On the tour one would pass many of the old inns including the Cot House Inn. This was built on the site of an ancient thatched cot-house in which resided the ferryman who kept the boat for crossing the Eachaig Water. In olden times it was the haunt of smugglers.

Nowadays you are more likely to meet some anglers. The Coylet Inn and Whistlefield Inn are also favourite haunts of anglers today. Behind Whistlefield a road goes over to Ardentinny while it was once possible to walk the five miles down Glenfinnart to catch a steamer to Dunoon.

Strachur lies on a small bay of Loch Fyne adjacent to the original point of the Creggan Ferry and five miles south of Inveraray. From this point the tourist gets an extensive view of the west side and also upper Loch Fyne as well as the range of mountains including Ben Cruachan.

In the summer of 1929 David Napier started a steam carriage service for the conveyance of passengers from Loch Eck to Creggans Ferry at Strachur. It went at a rate of 12mph on a hard surface, but was found to be useless on the soft sandy track found between Loch Eck and Loch Fyne. To the left of this view is the early 1920s equivalent, an early bus with solid rubber tyres. Fixed to the garage wall is a Michelin man.

The Columba, Grenadier and Chevalier in the graving dock at Govan for their spring refit.

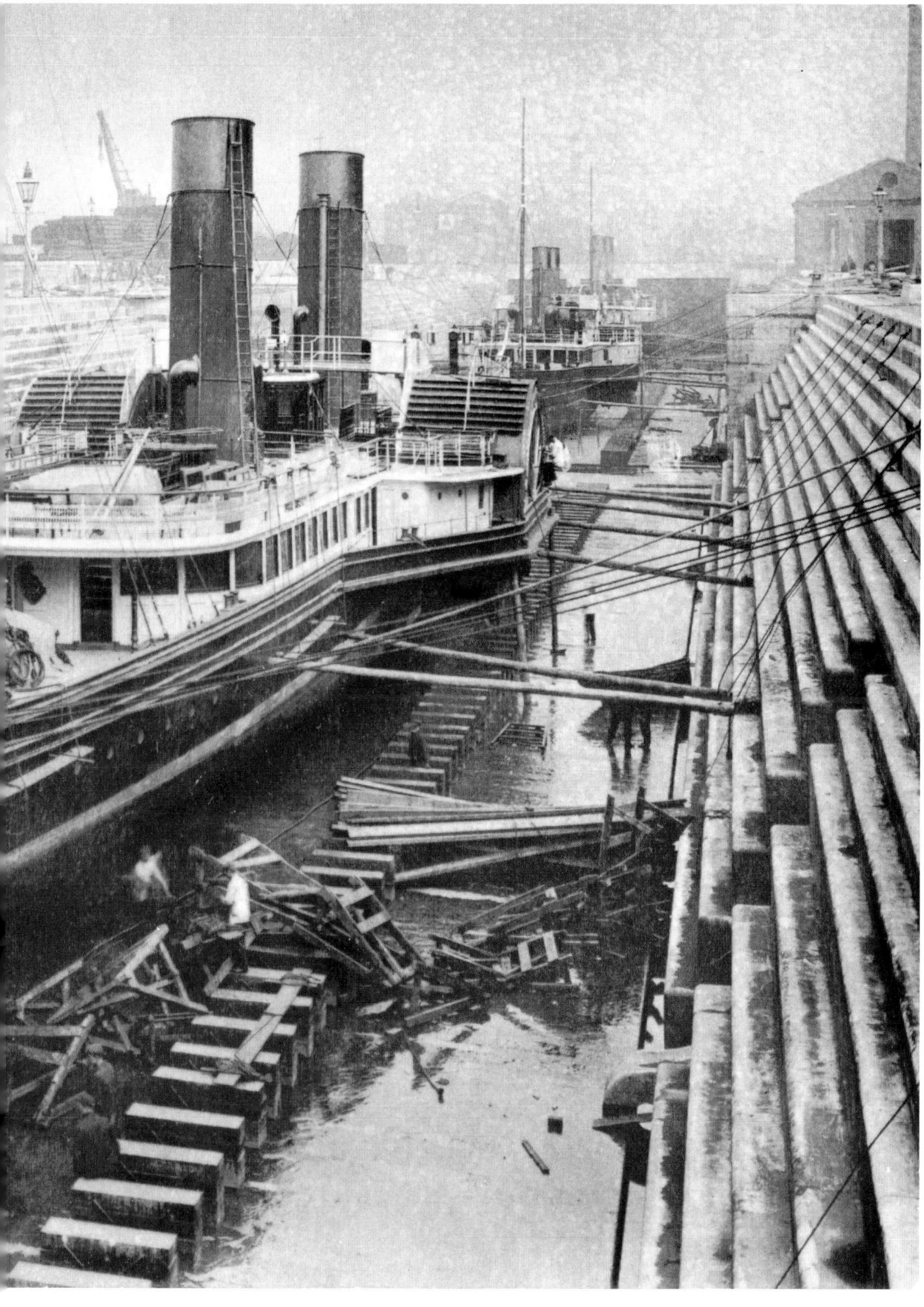

"Lord of the Isles". Strachur Pier.

Lord of the Isles ready to depart on the homeward bound trip back to Glasgow. Lord of the Isles sailed the route from Glasgow to Inveraray for twenty one years before she was retired as being too expensive in 1912. For another sixteen years she worked on other routes on the Clyde before being broken up in 1928.

This elephant and cart would have been a rare sight in any town at the turn of the century. The circus had arrived and would parade through the streets before setting up the big top. This scene of Inveraray dates from about 1905.

Loch Eck Tour Cars at Inveraray Pier   CS 702

By 1927 the Fairy Queen had gone from Loch Eck and the horse drawn coaches had been superseded by motor coaches such as Baird's Royal Blue Pullman coaches. This view of Inveraray dates from the mid 1920s and shows some of the motor cars used on the tours.

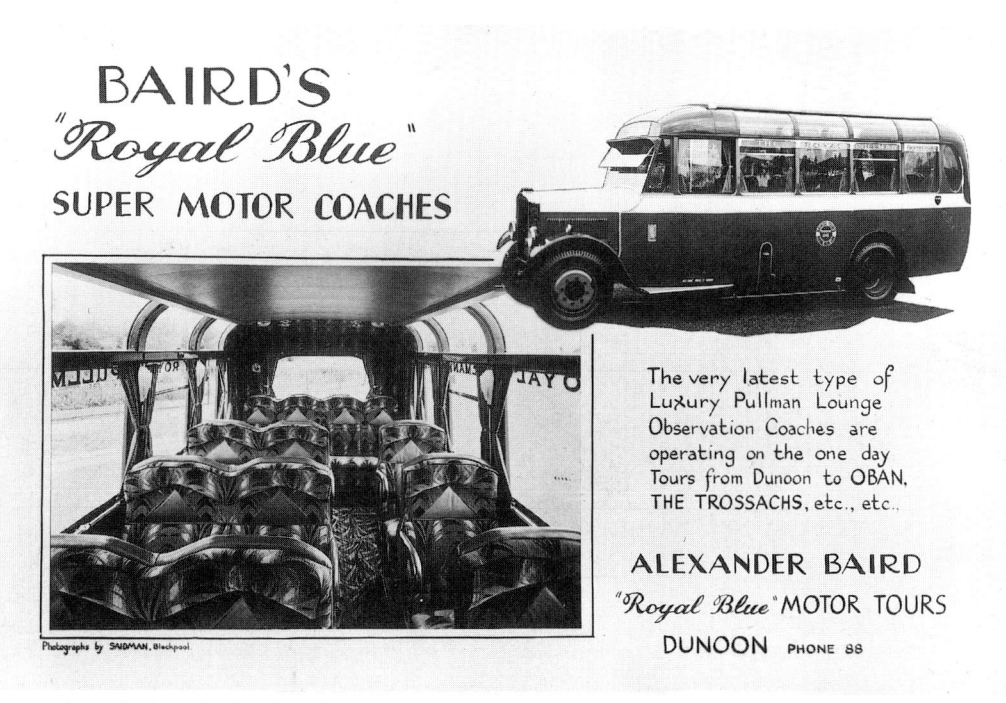

BAIRD'S "Royal Blue" SUPER MOTOR COACHES

The very latest type of Luxury Pullman Lounge Observation Coaches are operating on the one day Tours from Dunoon to OBAN, THE TROSSACHS, etc., etc..

ALEXANDER BAIRD
"Royal Blue" MOTOR TOURS
DUNOON   PHONE 88

Photographs by SNOMAN, Blackpool

The coaches which arrived only a few years later had extra panoramic windows fitted and many had full length folding canvas sunroofs. Tours were operated to Oban, the Trossachs via Loch Lomond, Ardentinny, Loch Striven and Loch Eck.

On the way to Rothesay the boats would stop at Craigmore, its charming suburb. The grand Victorian architecture of the villas is seen to good effect in this picture from 1923. Craigmore was favoured by people of substance such as the Glasgow businessmen who made good use of the fast steamers, then available, to commute. The pier closed in 1939 and was demolished the following year.

The pier administration buildings at Rothesay were constructed in 1885 and are Victorian grandeur at its best. The central clock tower with its rustic turrets is almost befitting of a fairy tale castle. This 1890s view gives some idea of the crowds coming off the boats. With arrivals and departures constantly, it made Rothesay a very hectic place to be on a summer weekend.

This view of the pier is taken from one of those many boats and gives some idea of the organisation needed to cater for the paddlers. Each boat required two or three gangways to let the passengers on and off as well as someone to take the pier dues for all arrivals and departures. Also in this view are some of the supplies that would have been carried by the boats to and from the island. First and foremost would have been enough food and drink to keep the holidaymakers happy.

Rothesay reigned as the Queen of the Clyde holiday resorts. It was the first watering place in Scotland to lay off an esplanade, to introduce a band, to provide proper bathing accommodation, to introduce electric light and the first to introduce electric tramways. Upwards of one hundred sailings per day made the choice of excursions practically unlimited. From the beginning of June till the end of August an average of 50,000 people were staying in the district in addition to the resident population.

They came to Rothesay for many reasons, not least the fact that the town offered the most varied entertainment. There was always something to do and these six scenes give an idea of what Victorian and early Edwardian Rothesay had to offer.

Almost before you were off the boat, there were all sorts of things to entice you along the esplanade. Visible from the pier would be some of the entertainers on the beach. This one, amazingly enough, managed to balance on the ladders, which is more than many of the tourists could manage after a visit to the nearest pub.

Any trip to the seaside would be incomplete without Punch & Judy and here they are playing to a large audience on Rothesay esplanade.

Another reason for coming was the shows. The small set up shows just some of the rides and side stalls. Just behind the small set of gallopers is a living van for the owners. Below is a set of swing boats on the esplanade.

Not everyone came to Rothesay for the entertainment.

43

Designed by local architect Andrew McKinley, the go-ahead for the new bandstand was given in 1911 here seen being opened later that same year. Little time was wasted between drawing board and completion. No doubt it was required for the summer visitors.

During August and September much of the town was illuminated and this view of an evening concert is probably taken sometime in one of these two months.

The Vulcan was originally intended to run on the route from Kilchattan Bay but was sold while still being built. Her first seven years were spent on excursion work along England's south coast. In 1904, she was sold to the Glasgow & South Western Railway who named her Vulcan and put her on the Fairlie to Millport run. This view shows the ship on a rare call to Kilchattan Bay.

Below is a 1930s view of Kilchattan Bay. Posted to Halifax in August 1938, the sender tells us that "this is a lovely place on a lovely day. We have just had tea and are sitting on the rocks, where I shall soon be really if I do not stop spending."

ROTHESAY & KYLES OF BUTE STEAMERS
SULTAN, SULTANA & VICEROY,
ALEX^r WILLIAMSON.

June 22nd
1883
Steamer Viceroy
Bridge Wharf
Glasgow

Dear Sir

Would kindly let me know at your earliest convenience the rate per ton for Steamer calling at Ardrishaig once or twice a week, also if we could have water for the Boiler

& Oblige
Yours respectfully
Alex Williamson

A letter from Alexander Williamson, owner of the Sultan, Sultana and Viceroy, to the Crinan Canal Office, Ardrishaig.

Here are the three boats of Williamson's Turkish Fleet. Berthed at Port Bannatyne, the Sultana (extreme right) is probably ready to set of for Glasgow on the first trip of the morning. In order to embark, passengers had to clamber over the other two steamers. They were sold in 1891 to the Glasgow & South Western Railway.

Port Bannatyne is next to Rothesay in size and about two and a half miles north of the latter. Originally known as Kamesburgh, this pretty little village set in Kames Bay is next to Kames Castle which was the home of the Bannatynes.

Sultan was built in 1861 by Barclay, Curle & Co. and was bought from McKellar by Alexander Williamson one year later. He placed her on the Glasgow to Rothesay route which she sailed for thirty years. When the Glasgow & South Western Railway acquired her, her name was changed to Ardmore. In 1895 she was sold to David MacBrayne for work on the Caledonian Canal. She was rebuilt with a new bow, new saloons and shortened by thirty feet, but her name was lengthened to Gairlochy. In 1919 she caught fire at Fort Augustus Pier and her keel is said to be still visible when the water level in Loch Ness is low.

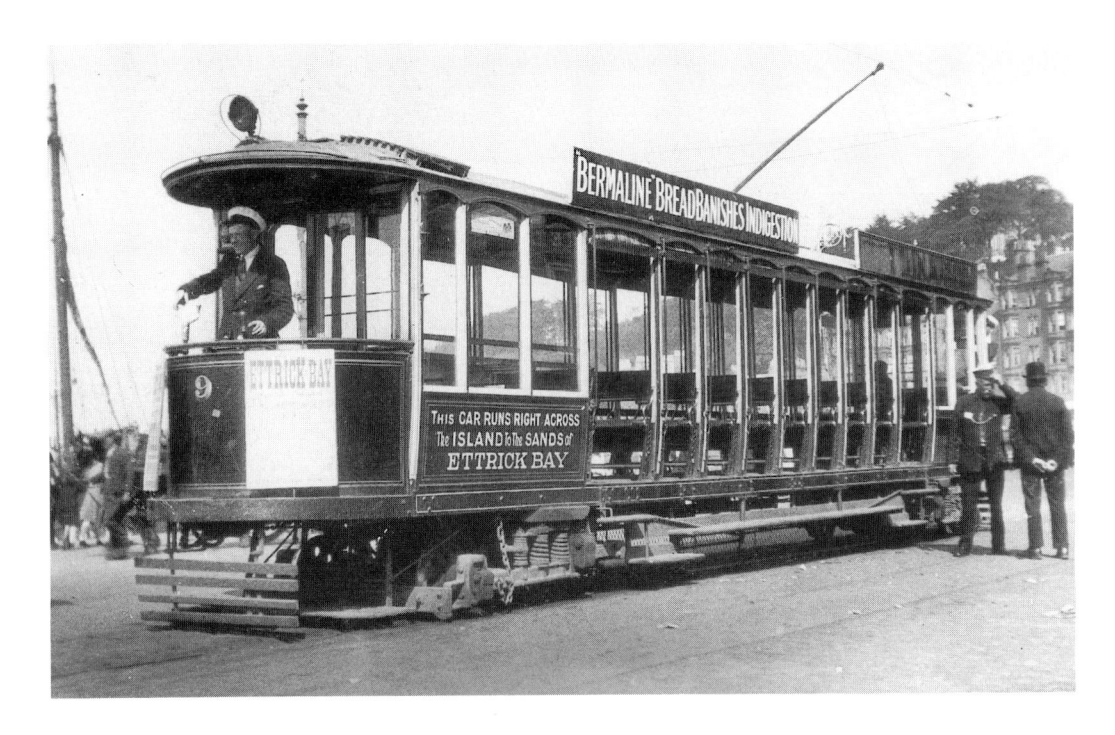

The old trams across the waist of Bute from Rothesay to Ettrick Bay were delightful in their time. The single deck vehicles were open at the sides and had hard wooden seats in a toast rack arrangement.

The trams would await the steamer at Port Bannatyne and travel across the island to the fine golden sands of Ettrick Bay. In 1912 this trip, including pier dues, cost 8d.

"The Lighthouse," Ettrick Bay Winning Sand Design.
International Sand Building Competition.

Town councils at the Clyde resorts organised sand castle building competitions usually twice per year. Hundreds of weans competed for the coveted prizes provided by the council. This example is from Ettrick Bay. The Daily Mail organised some of the International Competitions.

Another novel attraction at Ettrick Bay was a ride in a goat cart. At the turn of the century you could go for a trip along the beach in a wicker chair behind one of these poor goats.

Before the trams one way of getting across the island was by horse and coach. This four in hand coach has at least twenty two people on board.

Tighnabruaich Regatta CS

Beyond Rothesay are the famous Kyles of Bute. At first the channel is wide but just beyond Colintrave there seems to be barely room for the steamer to pass through. The small islets at the narrows are the Burnt Islands which are so called because of a vitrified fort on one. The name Tighnabruaich is Gaelic and means 'the house on the brae'. Tighnabruaich Pier served three small resorts. As well as Tighnabruaich, Auchenlochan and Kames were accessible from the pier.

The large steam yacht is the Iolaire which was built by Beardmores at Govan for William Birtwhistle.

R.M.S. COLUMBA AT TIGHNABRUAICH.

STEAMER AT TARBERT, LOCH FYNE.

The Columba was built in 1878 and served MacBrayne's well until 1935. She plied the same route from Glasgow to Ardrishaig except during the First World War when she sailed from Wemyss Bay because of the submarine boom.

At the pier head is Craig Brothers bus. They ran a service from Campbeltown to Tarbert carrying passengers and, at this time, mail in connection with the steamers.

S.S. "LINNET" AT DUNARDY LOCH, CRINAN CANAL.

Passengers continuing on beyond Tarbert would remain on board till the steamer reached Ardrishaig. There they would transfer to the canal steamer Linnet. Building of the Crinan Canal started in 1794 and it was intended to be a short cut for boats going to the islands. There were initial problems including that of attracting navvies to such a remote spot as well as problems after construction such as a reservoir collapsing in 1811.

Here is an example of the postmark used on the Columba. Other Clyde steamers, including the Chevalier, Grenadier and Iona, also had post offices on board. It meant that mail from the Isles, as well as Oban and Fort William, could be sorted en route.

The Columba was one of the most majestic ships sailing the lower reaches of the Clyde and holds a special place in the hearts of all who can remember her. At 301 feet she was the longest of all the Clyde steamers.

The Iona belonged to MacBraynes and was used on the Loch Fyne service until replaced by the Columba. As the Iona was too large to be used on the same route in the winter months, it was laid up at Bowling every autumn. The ship would leave Glasgow at 1.30pm and arrive at Ardrishaig at 7.15pm. She was reboilered in 1890 and lasted until 1937 when she was pensioned off after a long and useful life of seventy six years.

The Crinan Canal is 9 miles long and this is an account of an 1894 trip through the canal:

"Passengers are conveyed in a tiny but neat steamer (the Linnet) whose deck house, when crowded with tourists presents a curious appearance. She starts her journey at 1 o'clock and the distance is completed in two hours; one hour being entirely taken up by delays at nine locks (out of a total of fifteen) through which we pass. During these stoppages most people get out and walk, re-joining the boat at the last lock. For the first one and a half miles the boat skirts the bay of Loch Gilp. At its head is Lochgilphead, a watering place. In half an hour we reach Cairnbaan Inn (four miles) where the coach road to Loch Awe strikes north. Locks in rapid succession now occur. Those who prefer to walk can do so and re-join the steamer at Lock 8. Having passed the summit level (five miles) we descend to the Atlantic."

The Linnet connected with the steamers to Oban and the Isles at Crinan. From the terminus of the canal steamer, half a minute's walk took you to the pier and the awaiting ship. The Chevalier was the most commonly used ship on the Crinan half of the Royal Route. From Crinan she would sail up the coast stopping at Oban, Ballachulish, Fort William and then Corpach. Most of the passengers, however, would either join or leave the boat at Oban for the connections to the Islands.

The Chevalier was built in 1866 at Clydebank and used mainly on West Highland services until 1913. During the First World War she was used on the Wemyss Bay to Rothesay or Millport runs. During refitting at Greenock in 1919 she caught fire but the damage was limited and she re-entered service on summer runs to Ardrishaig. In March 1927 a paddle broke and the ship ran aground on rocks near to Barmore Island in Loch Fyne. After being towed to Troon it was discovered that the Chevalier was beyond economic repair and as a result she was scrapped.

At Oban Pier, Steamer " Grenadier " (with Steam up) for Staffa and Iona. Steamer " Chevalier " for Crinan.

From the summer of 1886 the cruises to Staffa and Iona were the domain of the MacBrayne paddle steamer Grenadier. Her summer visits on the Sacred Isle Cruise offered passengers one and a half hours ashore. Her annual routine was sailing from Greenock and Ardrishaig between October and March and from June till September she cruised from Oban to Staffa and Iona. In September 1927 she caught fire at the pier at Oban and three of her crew, including the captain, were killed. Her last voyage was in April 1928 from Greenock to Ardrossan for scrapping.

Being a good sea boat the Grenadier was requisitioned as a minesweeper during World War One and was renamed HMS Grenade. After a refit she rejoined her old routes. This 1900s view shows her at Staffa.

P. S. Columba

S.S. "Kenilworth"

FIRTH OF CLYDE, SCOTLAND. (1)

*Yon wild, mossy mountains sae lofty and wide,
That swell with their torrents the might of the Clyde.*

THE "PREMIER" SERIES, No 1951. (COPYRIGHT)

---

*The land o' the loch and the river,
The land o' the ben and the brae,*

FIRTH OF CLYDE, SCOTLAND. (2)

Thanks for letter & enclosure. Will send on box early next week. With love from A.B.

THE "PREMIER" SERIES, 1952 (COPYRIGHT)

CALEDONIAN RAILWAY
Excursion Programme
TO THE COAST
"DUCHESS OF HAMILTON"
TRAINS Run on to PIER Alongside STEAMERS
VIA
ARDROSSAN
WEMYSS BAY
& GOUROCK

Summer Tours in the
Western
ROYAL ROUTE
of
BY THE
ROYAL MAIL STEAMERS
Columba,
DAVID MACBRAYNE
T. FORMAN & SONS, DESIGNERS

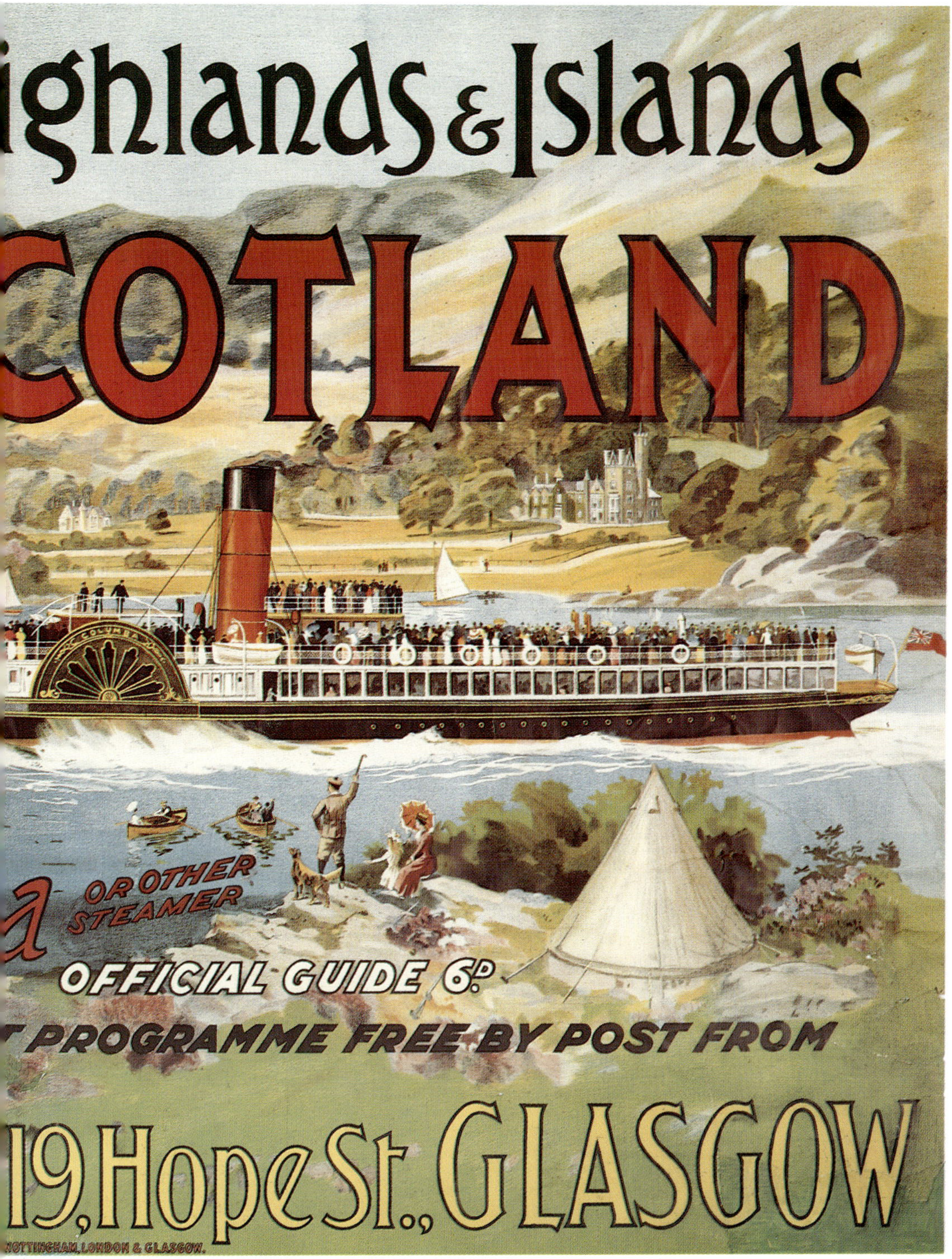
ighlands & Islands
COTLAND
a OR OTHER STEAMER
OFFICIAL GUIDE 6D
PROGRAMME FREE BY POST FROM
19, Hope St., GLASGOW
NOTTINGHAM, LONDON & GLASGOW.

"IN THE GOOD OLD SUMMER TIME"
"FAITHER" CATCHES A CRAB.

"IN THE GOOD OLD SUMMER TIME"
MERCY ME! WHIT IF WE'RE LEFT HERE A' NICHT
THE LAST BOAT
PIER DUES
SEA
SAILING
THE FAST S

"SEASIDE."

PA AND MA COME ASHORE AT LOW TIDE AFTER A SAIL.

An Evening Cruise

MAGNIFICENT NEW TURBINE STEAMERS
Pleasure Sailing on the FIRTH of CLYDE.

on Board
S.S. *Alexandrina*
26/5/03

Having a good old time here hope to see you soon from yer bit quite

Goatfell   Whiting Bay

Caledonian Steamer,

64

The Claymore was built expressly for the Skye and Stornoway route and had splendid passenger accommodation. The 1881 MacBraynes guidebook states that the "tourist can thus obtain a pleasant trip by leaving Glasgow any Monday or Thursday in the Claymore for Stornoway, via Mull of Kintyre going and returning through the Sounds of Jura, Mull and Skye. Calling at Oban, Tobermory, Portree and intermediate amongst scenery rich in variety and loveliness. By this means a weeks most enjoyable pleasure sailing (remaining on board the steamer during the nights) may be had. Cabin fare for the round trip 45 shillings; including meals 80 shillings." For £4 I'd have been expecting to sit at the Captain's table with the other three officers!

By 1902 the Week's Tour to Stornoway was now calling at Kyle of Lochalsh with its magnificent pier and terminus of the Dingwall & Skye section of the Highland Railway. Here passengers who had come by train from the south would embark.

Oban, the capital of Lorne, command one of the grandest views of island and sea scenery in Western Scotland. It is still a great tourist and yachting centre and was once one of the most fashionable watering places. A natural gateway to the west, Oban began to grow in the early 19th Century with a doubling of its population from 600 to 1500 as shipbuilding and farming developed. The town became a burgh in 1811. Piers were built and sailings to the Western Isles and Lorne were greatly increased, but the new Oban was given its biggest boost by the arrival of steam boats in the 1850s. The arrival of the Callander & Oban Railway in 1880 gave further impetus for an increased tourist trade. The town has never looked back.

With the coming of the various railways it was possible to go on round trip tours using a variety of different forms of transport. The Callander & Oban made possible tours to the Trossachs as well as the Western Isles possible in a shorter time as well as being cheaper than the all boat trips. Here a crowd of tourists await the train to the north in 1904.

King Edward was the first turbine steamer on the Clyde coast services. The ship was built in 1901 at Denny's shipyard in Dumbarton and had a coal fired boiler and three direct drive turbines. Used on the Greenock to Campbeltown service, King Edward was so successful that a larger sister ship was built the following year. In 1951 King Edward was laid up and scrapped shortly afterwards.

The Queen Alexandra was just a little longer than the King Edward and two knots faster. A problem with her propellers led to her being transferred from her original owner, Captain James Williamson, and she was bought by Turbine Steamers Ltd. Used as a consort to King Edward, she was the fastest ship on the Clyde with a top speed of 21 knots. Fire broke out when she was coaling at Greenock. Although not a total loss, the ship was repaired and sold to the Canadian Pacific Railway. She sailed to Vancouver, was renamed the Princess Patricia, and was withdrawn in 1937.

During her period with the Glasgow & Inveraray Steamboat Co. the Lord of the Isles was used on the Glasgow to Inveraray run. After being purchased by Turbine Steamers Ltd in 1912, she was placed on the Tighnabruaich run via Bute.

The railway to Fairlie opened in June 1880 and the last link to the pier opened just over a year later. Fairlie was well placed for serving Millport and offered the shortest sea crossing from the Clyde coast to Campbeltown. Fast trains ran direct from Glasgow to Fairlie Pier. In 1902, when the Queen Alexandra was put on the service, the King Edward was used on excursions to Inveraray. The top view shows a Glasgow & South Western Railway 4-4-0 at Fairlie Station while the bottom view, of 1904, shows the King Edward at Fairlie Pier.

A Stormy Day off Ardrossan; Steamer "Duchess of Hamilton"
We expect Nancy here on Saturday. CBC. 18th, 7th, 1906.

Here we have two of the Caledonian Steam Packet Company's finest steamers, the Duchess of Hamilton (above) and Duchess of Argyll (below). Competition with the Glasgow & South Western Railway was fierce and this gave the people of Arran a wonderful service from Ardrossan. The Steam Packet Co. was an offshoot of the Caledonian Railway and gave the South Western's steamers as much competition at sea as the railways gave on land. Posted at Skelmorlie, the sender of the above card says "This is the kind of weather we are having here at present. Father was on this boat when the photo was taken two years ago, when we were at Whiting Bay".

The Duchess of Argyll was the first turbine steamer for the Company and appeared in 1906. She is seen here at Montgomerie Pier sometime before 1910.

Ardrossan Harbour.

At the northern crescent of Lamlash Bay is the hamlet of King's Cross. This area has historical associations with Robert the Bruce. Here he took refuge in a cave when his cause was faltering and awaited the call from Ayrshire to continue his work of freeing Scotland.

The slightly hazardous and time consuming operation of ferrying passengers and their luggage to the steamers from the landing stage can be seen to good effect in these two pictures of Glasgow & South Western Railway steamers.

The Landing Stage, Kings Cross, Arran

70

Lamlash shared the Arran holiday trade with Brodick. Guarding the entrance to the bay is Holy Isle which created an excellent haven for the Channel Fleet. This postcard view was used in 1912 from HMS Hibernia. The writer informs us that "the first pilot in the world to take off in an aeroplane from a ship underway" took off from this ship in May 1912 at Portland.

Compare this photograph taken some 66 years later with the above. It shows the Waverley during September 1978 off Lamlash pierhead. Replacing the Channel Fleet is an oil rig. The Waverley made the first big ship call to Lamlash in forty years in May 1994.

ROYAL MAIL ROUTE VIA KILBRANNAN SOUND TO CAMPBELTOWN.

CAPTAIN N. MACALISTER.

CAPTAIN P. McFARLANE.

TWICE DAILY IN SUMMER.

R.M.S. KINLOCH.

R.M.S. DAVAAR.

The Glasgow & Campbeltown Steam Packet Co. owned three ships, SS Kintyre, SS Kinloch and SS Davaar. All three were built for the Glasgow To Campbeltown route via Lochranza, Pirnmill and Carradale.

The Kintyre (seen here at Lochranza) was the first of their boats and was built in 1868 at Port Glasgow. The yacht-like boat had clipper bows and a well-raked funnel. The Kinloch was as much a freight boat as a passenger one and as a result did not always run to schedule. It was common to see her loaded with fish crates, sheep or whisky piled high on board.

In 1907 she was rammed by the steamer Maori, then on her speed trials. The two ships were locked together long enough for the passengers to leap from the Kinloch but the ship sank only a few minutes after they broke loose.

Built in 1878 at Pointhouse, the Kinloch was a slightly larger version of the Kintyre but still retained the yacht like looks of her predecessor. She was as up to date as possible and her design led to rapid handling of cargo and passengers. In 1926 she was sold to new owners in the Channel Islands and broken up at Bowness two years later.

Carradale Pier was said to be the first in Scotland to be made of iron and dated from 1872. The Post Office at Carradale Pier opened in January 1898 and this postcard view was posted from there only seven years later. The Post Office closed in June 1941, just over a year after the last passenger ship called at the pier. The Waverley called at the pier in September 1992 and was the first passenger ship to do so for forty two years.

The Davaar was built in 1885 and replaced the Gael in the Campbeltown & Glasgow Steam Packet company's fleet. As originally built she had twin funnels but was reboilered in 1903. For most of her life she served Campbeltown from various ports but when on a cruise to Belfast in 1895 she ran aground in fog. All her passengers were taken ashore but it took two days to refloat her. She was used as a blockship at Newhaven to prevent the Germans using the harbour in any invasion of the south of England. With the threat of invasion over, she was scrapped in 1943.

This view is of Torpedo Boat No.13. Not one of the Navy's luckiest boats, it ran aground in Campbeltown Loch in 1910. This picture was taken only a day or so after the disaster and shows some of the crew and other navy personnel deciding how to refloat her.

The first railway at Campbeltown was constructed in 1876 and was to serve the colliery near Machrihanish. Only coal trains ran on it but the coming of the turbine steamers in 1901 changed all that. During the summers of 1901-3 over 130,000 visitors came to the town. Of these, 22,000 were booked through to Machrihanish. It was an ideal opportunity for the railway owners to make some money. The line was expanded and rebuilt to take passengers. In 1907 it opened for traffic and was an instant success. By the 1930s, competition from buses had killed the railway though and it closed in 1932.

As well as the railway to Machrihanish, it was possible to spend an afternoon exploring Campbeltown's quaint old back streets. This view shows the Wide Close and some of its inhabitants sometime at the turn of the century.

FERRY LEAVING PIRNMILL.

Pirnmill takes its name from the mill established there by an enterprising Paisley merchant. This mill made pirns (reels or spools for thread) from the plentiful local birch wood. This snug little hamlet, with its healthy and breezy land above, was frequented by Glasgow folk during the summer months seeking recuperation from their weary days spent in the smoke filled city.

"Just down here for the day on the Turbine Steamer Queen Alexandra. The morning was lovely but it has rained since my arrival here. One of these nice gentle Arran showers which never goes off".

One can envisage the writer of this postcard climbing down from the steamer into a rowing boat, being ferried to the small wooden landing stage and then being asked to clamber over the rocks.

This view of the Moorings dates from 1936. Opposite the entrance is a Clyde Coast Services bus. The driver is standing at the front nearside in his white dust coat. Largs was a popular excursion port of call for the steamers and it was possible to visit most places on the Clyde from there during the summer.

No trip to Largs could be complete without a visit to Nardinis.

German Gypsies and their dancing bear at Largs on a dreich winter day. In the first decade of this century, dancing bears were something that you would have seen at least once in many of the larger towns. The bear was muzzled and chained and would be made to dance for the entertainment of those tasteless enough to want to watch.

Leaving Largs about 1910 is one of the Caledonian Steam Packet Company's boats.

In 1905 Millport Town Council purchased the old pier at Millport from the Marquis of Bute for £5030 as well as Keppel Pier for £2000. This picture shows the pier as it was owned by the Marquis of Bute.

This 1920s view of the Glen Rosa shows many of the improvements made by the Council to the pier, including at the pier end the red signal cabin with its distinctive turreted roof and the clock at the turnstiles presented by Provost Cockburn. Pier dues in this 1920s view were 2d per passenger. It wasn't until the 1960s that the dues were included in the ticket price.

A view of one of the entrants in the sand castle building competition at Millport in August 1913.

Keppel Pier, Millport sometime between 1904 and 1908. The pier is now long gone.

Harvesting, Hunterston Estate, West Kilbride.

West Kilbride was a pleasant holiday haunt and a place of rest. With its Co-operative Home and the Hydro at nearby Seamill as well as other rest homes, it was an ideal place for one recovering from illness.

A few miles up the coast from West Kilbride is Portencross, a hamlet at the most westerly point of Ayrshire. Next to the castle was a Spanish Armada cannon which has since been moved to Hunterston B Power Station. After the Armada was routed by the English Navy, it sailed round the north of Scotland on its long sail back to Spain via Ireland. Many ships did not make it past the Scottish coast as the English Fleet, war damage and our weather got them in the autumn of 1588.

The pier at Portencross was built in 1912 and is referred to in T C F Brotchie's book - Western Holiday Haunts - as just being built. This view shows the Juno on an excursion from Ayr. She was built in 1898 and was based at Ayr for sailings to Arran. A weekly trip was also made to Stranraer. She was commandeered in 1914 by the Admiralty and named HMS Junior. Juno always used a lot of coal and was never economical. Her last owners, the London, Midland & Scottish Railway, sent her to Alloa for breaking up in 1931.

A view of the Throughlet looking to Northbank Cottage dating from sometime around 1908. After leaving the pier, one could spend a good two or three hours touring the local countryside.

A policeman stands on guard outside Northbank on the 19th of October, 1913. The night before, Miss Mary Gunn was shot while knitting. She died almost instantly. Her sister was shot twice but survived and her brother in law lost his finger in the attack. It was a dark, stormy night and the assailant escaped and was never brought to justice.

Built in 1892, the Glen Sannox was the fastest ship on the Clyde at one point with a top speed of over 20 knots. Most of her life was spent on the run to Brodick but occasionally she would be seen on excursion trips. When running at top speed, her boilers were very heavy on coal and this was a deciding factor in her being scrapped in 1925.

For nearly a century and a half Saltcoats thrived on the salt trade, but by the time these pictures were taken it was the salt air blowing off the Clyde that the town thrived on. It had become a fashionable watering place and had gained a reputation for being bright and pretty in appearance and healthy to live in.

As well as donkey rides along the beach and walks along the promenade, it was possible to idle away a few hours at the harbour side fishing or watching the boats. In the background can be seen the Pavilion where shows were hosted throughout the summer.

One of the great attractions at Saltcoats was Harry Kemp's Scotch Broth. For much of the 1920s and 1930s, they gave shows in the La Scala.

Chancellor and Sultan.

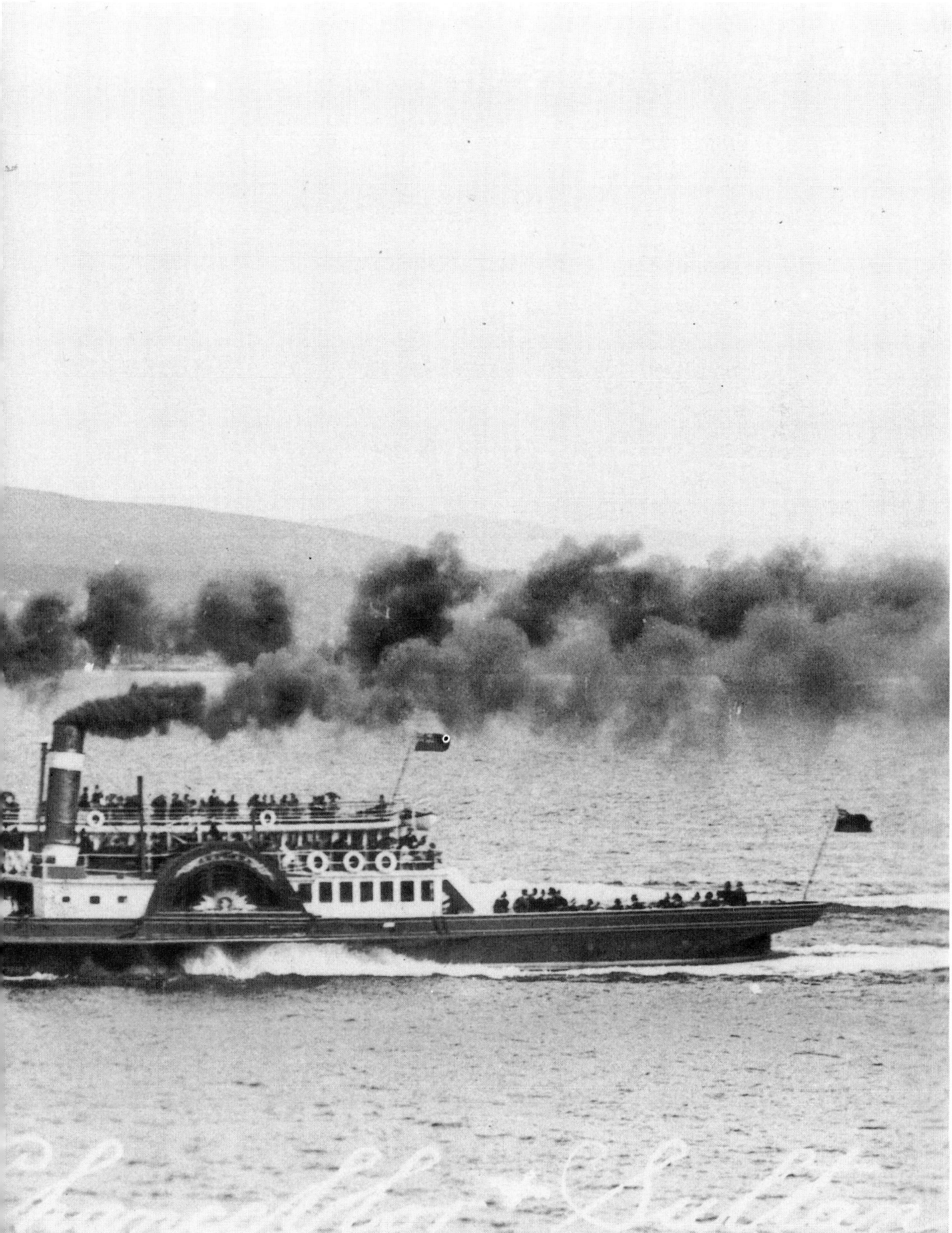

Troon, with its golf courses (one of Championship standard) and fine beaches, became the permanent home of many of Glasgow's well to do businessmen. This view shows Troon's natural harbour formed by its promontory and further developed by the Duke of Portland with the completion of sea walls, piers and breakwaters. The railway to Troon was opened in 1812 from Kilmarnock and was the first proper railway in Scotland. Steam trains were introduced in 1817.

In this view a boat is being coaled. Some ports had automatic coaling machines but this picture shows a wagon being hoisted by a crane and tipped.

The Juno at Troon. Amidships, the travellers are being entertained by one of the German bands that were popular before the start of the First World War. In the background are rows of coal wagons fanning out from the graving dock.

On the Sands, Ayr.

Ayr was and still is a favourite with working folk around the Clyde who enjoyed good lodgings, beaches, putting greens, municipal golf courses and entertainment. The latter was provided at the town's various theatres including the Gaiety, which opened in 1902, and the Ayr Pavilion which dates from 1911 and has shown all sorts of entertainment including boxing, pop concerts and cinema. Part of the building is now used by the rave club Hangar 13.

HARBOUR, AYR.

The harbour at Ayr underwent great improvements between 1874-78 at a cost of £200,000 and eventually became the domain of the Glasgow & South Western Railway. The excursion trade was operated by the likes of the Juno and Glen Sannox.

Glasgow. Do you recognise this spot. Queen Street. Station.
The Wrench Series, No. 7636

Horse cabs and lorries gather at the entrance to Queen Street Station. From the low level station, a journey of about an hour brings the holidaymaker to Craigendoran. The moment the train emerges from the Queen Street Tunnel, the Clyde comes into view and it is followed all the way.

On the way one would see the Singer Factory at Clydebank, one of the largest factories in the world as well as pass over the Forth & Clyde Canal.

Helensburgh. S.S. "Lucy Ashton" Craigendoran Pier.

From the pier at Craigendoran the North British Railway's palatial steamers started on their excursions to places as far away as Ardrishaig.

The West Highland and North British Railways met about a mile from Helensburgh. It was originally intended to run the North British direct to the Helensburgh pier and erect a station there but the town objected. Afraid of the loss of trade to local shopkeepers, they kept the NB from the pier. The railway then built a pier at Craigendoran in 1882. It closed in 1972 and was the home of the Waverley till it closed.

A view of the pier at Helensburgh with the Lucy Ashton present. She was built in 1888 and maintained the services to Dunoon and Holy Loch. When the railways were amalgamated in 1923, she was taken under the control of the London & North Eastern Railway who reboilered her. In 1949 she was sent to Faslane for scrapping but her hull was taken to Dumbarton for experimental work. The boat was fitted with two Rolls Royce jet engines and used for research and development. After two years she was taken back to Faslane and scrapped.

There are six or seven Campbeltown registered herring boats in this view of Helensburgh dating from the 1930s.

FIRST FLYWHEEL OF THE "COMET" HERMITAGE PARK, HELENSBURGH. HLGS. 25.

It was on the Clyde, in 1812, that the Comet firmly inaugurated steam navigation in Europe. The owner of this little craft was Henry Bell who was born at Torphichen Mill, near Linlithgow, in 1767 and died at Helensburgh in 1830.

Helensburgh owes much to Bell. He came to the town in 1808 and became tenant of the Baths Hotel. He was also first Provost of the town and helped greatly in promoting it as a tourist resort.

The Comet was built by John Wood & Co, Port Glasgow, and made its first trip to Glasgow on 6th August, 1812. Thereafter the boat plied between Glasgow and Greenock with the odd foray to Helensburgh. She moved to Grangemouth for a few years but returned to the Clyde in 1819. In December 1820 the Comet ran aground near Crinan and the passengers and crew managed to scramble ashore. Travelling down the Clyde today it is possible to see two monuments to Bell, one at Helensburgh and the other at Bowling.

LNER

Afternoon Excursion

TO THE

KYLES OF BUTE

BY STEAMER

"MARMION"

OR OTHER STEAMER

Daily

FROM 13TH JUNE TO 10TH SEPTEMBER

From	Going	Returning	Return Fares. Cabin	Return Fares. Steerage
	p.m.	p.m.	S. D.	S. D.
Helensburgh*	depart 12 15	arrive 7†12		
Craigendoran	,, 12 32	,, 6 40	3 9	3 0
Kilcreggan	,, 12 48	,, 6 20		
Kirn	,, 1 3	,, 6s5		
Dunoon	,, 1 10	,, 6 0	3 0	2 3
Innellan	,, 1 30	,, 5 40		
Craigmore	,, 1 50	,, 5 20	1 6	1 0
Rothesay	,, 2 15	,, 5 5		
Tighnabruaich	arrive 2 55	depart 4 15	...	...
Auchenlochan	,, 3 0	,, 4 10	...	...
Kames	,, 3 5	,, 4 5		

* Steamer may not call at Helensburgh at low tide.

† Saturdays only June and September: Daily July and August.

s Saturdays only.

Passengers have an hour ashore at Tighnabruaich, Auchenlochan or Kames.

May 1927   (10-M)   S.C. 4397

Hugh Paton & Sons, Ltd., Printers, Edinburgh

To visit this district without sailing through the Kyles of Bute would be to miss one of the finest journeys in the world.

The Marmion was built in 1906 and was designed for year round use. She cruised to Loch Long, Loch Goil, Rothesay and the Kyles of Bute as well as excursions to Largs, served in both wars and made three trips to Dunkirk. During the night of the 8th-9th April, 1941 she was hit during an air raid at Harwich and sunk in the harbour.

The shallow water at Craigendoran meant that the North British was still building paddlers when some of the other fleets had turned to screw propelled ships.

Row, from Gareloch.

Some two miles from Helensburgh lies the village of Row. The North British Railway owned the pier and railway station here. Henry Bell, of Comet fame, is buried here and a few miles further on, at Shandon, was the former home of the equally famous shipbuilder and engineer, Robert Napier.

At the pier the Lucy Ashton. On the Gareloch route, she would have been calling at Helensburgh, Rosneath, Clynder, Shandon, Rahane Ferry, Mambeg and Garelochhead as well as Row and Craigendoran.

Garelochhead. 393/23

Stretching away to the right of Rosneath, inland among the hills, is the Gareloch, where ships anchored and adjusted their compasses. At the end of this stretch of inland sea is Garelochhead. The village lies just over seven miles north west of Helensburgh and shown in this view of the pier is Lady Clare.

Built in Paisley, Lady Clare was completed in 1891 and was used for short runs from Craigendoran. Displaced by the Marmion, she was sold in 1906 and ended up on Lough Foyle in Ireland until she was scrapped in 1928.

A July day in the 1900s.

The steamer from Craigendoran rounds Rosneath Point and between Gareloch and Loch Long is the delightful holiday spot of Kilcreggan. It stands opposite Gourock and, by sea, is three and a half miles north west of Greenock. At the pier is the Mars, of the Glasgow & South Western Railway. Requisitioned during the First World War and named HMS Marsa, she was involved in a collision at Harwich and sank in 1918.

"Waverley" and "Iona" at Arrochar Pier.

At the head of Loch Long is the picturesque resort of Arrochar. The district is rich in natural beauty for it must be remembered that Arrochar is only two miles from Tarbet on Loch Lomond. Ben Arthur, better known as the Cobbler, rises to close on 3000 feet, a spectacular backdrop for any picture of a steamer at the pier.

The mountainous estate of 9000 acres between Loch Goil and Loch Long is known as Argyll's Bowling Green and was gifted to the people of Glasgow by A. Cameron Corbett as a place for recreation.

Carrick Castle dates from the early 15th Century and adds romance to the day tripper's search for peace and quiet. This sentiment is echoed by the sender of these postcard views on 15th July 1912, who writes "The best day's sailing I have ever had up Loch Goil. The sun was shining even on the water and was like a body alive. There was about fourteen tents camped here, nearly all married couples with families".

This view shows the Edinburgh Castle with a list to port as passengers prepare to land at Carrick Pier.

The village of Lochgoilhead extends half round the curve of the loch, at its head a remote area on the shores of the Clyde surrounded by mountain scenery, and a pleasing sight to the visitor. Down through the years it was well served by steamers and the day tripper could spend an hour or two exploring the beauty of the place. These two 1900s views show the boat station, where rowing boats could be hired and the view from the pier.

The Edinburgh Castle first saw service on the Clyde in 1879. She was built at Port Glasgow by R Duncan and was the third ship in the fleet of the Lochgoil & Loch Long Steamboat Company. In 1888 she was used in an experiment to try out patent briquettes as a fuel source and as a means of cutting down smoke. The experiment was a great success but the ship's fuel consumption increased and the trial was discontinued. For all of her thirty three year life she sailed on the route from Glasgow to Lochgoilhead and was scrapped in 1913.

Just one of the mishaps which bedevilled the Grenadier. In November 1907 she ran aground in dense fog and was holed.

99

One of the best built for the Caledonian Steam Packet Company, the Duchess of Rothesay lasted through two world wars to complete 50 years of service. She was the first paddler built by Thomson's for the Caley and did that yard proud. Much of her life was spent on the Arran run but she was a popular excursion boat. She earned a unique claim to fame in the First World War by towing a wrecked German Zeppelin back to port after it had come down in the North Sea and been captured.

While being refitted for passenger service after the war, someone left a sea cock open and the ship sank at her moorings. It was a few weeks later when she could be raised and the refit finished. She was requisitioned again in 1939. In 1945 she was considered uneconomic to repair and scrapped in Holland.

The Queen Alexandra at Gourock Pier sometime about 1905.